Praise for Michael Casey

"The publication of Michael Casey's *There It Is: New & Selected Poems*, with his quirky portraits of ordinary Americans, is an event to celebrate. Like a photographer snapping pictures relentlessly, he must have written a poem about everyone he ever met with dead-on realism. Compared to him, the *Spoon River Anthology* is a work for kiddies. If Robert Frost was a poet of the rural New Englander, Michael Casey, also a New Englander, brings to life his mill town background, the guys who didn't go on to college and the larger world, but married the girls they dated in high school and got jobs in the mill. When he's sent to Vietnam he captures his fellow soldiers in their own military jargon. A master of the vernacular, he forces one to question writing in the 'correct' language when so many of us speak it quite differently, the language we think and feel in. Rare among poets, he's willing to explore colloquial speech in all its messiness, and gets it down perfectly – in fact, he's got us all down spot on. This collection, with its wide range of voices, is a unique achievement."
— **Edward Field**, author of *The Man Who Would Marry Susan Sontag* and *After the Fall: Poems Old and New*

"I first heard Michael Casey read some of these poems on a July evening in New Hampshire long ago while the war in Vietnam was still a tremendous confusion and sorrow for all of us and the poems made sense of it in a new way. My writer father had discovered that our summer neighbor was a poet and had invited him to read to us. I was stunned by the power of the language, the great-heartedness of the poems, the way Casey was not afraid to write about how men act under pressure, the way he used ordinary words to describe extraordinary feelings.

Now I read the poems in a New York City apartment in a time that seems as confusing as the 1970's. Michael Casey's poems changed as he went back to work after the war and later when he moved north, but their power is undiminished. He is tough but the poems are tender. These are poems that grab you by the heart and refuse to let you go. Read them!"
– **Susan Cheever**, author of *Drinking in America: Our Secret History* and *E.E. Cummings: A Life*

"There is an accomplished art concealed in Mr. Casey's seemingly offhand sketches."
— **Daniel Hoffman**, *The New York Times*

"The man has that rare sense of language alive, each word as important to test against each other before letting it stay as every other word you keep."
— **Nat Hentoff**, *The Village Voice*

There It Is: New & Selected Poems
by Michael Casey

© 2017 by Michael Casey
All Rights Reserved

ISBN 978-093150742-7
Printed in the U.S.A.
First Edition

Design: Kelly Freitas
Cover Image: "Mill-City Cityscape" by Denis Tangney Jr.
Author Photograph: Katherine Casey
Typeface: Adobe Garamond Pro text and Franklin Gothic display
Printing: King Printing

Loom Press
P.O. Box 1394
Lowell, MA 01853
www.loompress.com

King Printing Co., Inc.
181 Industrial Ave. East
Lowell, MA 01852
www.kingprinting.com

Many of these poems, sometimes in different versions, first appeared in the follow-
ing books and chapbooks: *Obscenities, Millrat, The Million Dollar Hole, Raiding a
Whorehouse, Permanent Party, Cindi's Fur Coat, The Bopper, The Wall Board Knife,*
and *Check Point*s.

I thank the editors of the following publications for originally printing the poems
of this book and for their allowing the poems to be included in this collection:
*Aisling; America; The Amherst Review; Ararat; The Birmingham Poetry Review; Boston
Phoenix; Ethos; 5 A.M.; California Quarterly; The Coe Review; Colere; The Common
Ground Review; Exempla; Fence; Gargoyle; Harvard Magazine; The Hat; Hospital
Drive; Ibbetson Street Review; J Journal; Jimson Weed; Ladowich; The Larcom Review;
The Listening Eye; Measurements: Out of Buffalo; The Mid-America Poetry Review;
The Minnesota Review; Model Homes; Nantucket Review; The Nation; The New Ohio
Review; The New Salt Creek Reader; The New York Times; The Panhandler; Pome-
granate Press Broadside Series; Prairie Schooner; The Purchase Poetry Review; Rolling
Stone; Salmagundi; Schist; Slow Loris Press Broadside Series; Square Lake; Stringtown;
Pavement Saw; War, Literature, and the Arts; Veterans for Peace;* and *Writers' Monthly.*

There It Is

New & Selected Poems

Also by Michael Casey

Obscenities
Millrat
The Million Dollar Hole
Raiding a Whorehouse
Permanent Party
Cindi's Fur Coat
The Bopper
The Wall Board Knife
Check Points

There It Is

New & Selected Poems

Michael Casey

Loom Press
Lowell, Massachusetts

For William Aiken

Contents

5

6

the last Yankee

she would walk around Centralville
with grocery bags with string handles
looking into garbage cans
in winter not so much for food
as for fuel
wood, newspaper, cardboard
and pieces of old furniture
for a black kitchen stove
I helped her get into her house once
when she forgot her key
had to break a cellar window
and climb through
while she stood outside
pretending her bags
were filled with groceries
she said the City of Lowell
made an offer to give her
so much a month if only
she'd sign over the house
the owner of the Irish nursing home
tried a similar deal too
but she didn't like the idea
the politicians and nursing home owner
were trying to steal her house
and she wanted me to understand
that two things ruined this town
unions and Catholics
they took over city hall
and the mills
and now they wanted her home

grandfather's photograph

there he is with Frankie
Frankie was a corporal in the Marines
and he had his picture taken with Frankie
but it bothered him
that Frankie wasn't an officer
none of his sons became officers
and it bothered him sore
I don't know what's wrong with all of them
every other family has an officer
he was getting old then
and this troubled him
he was Irish
and wanted to be proud of his sons

The Marlborough

for Martin Moriarty

it used to be a nice hotel
my big sister married there
but before that
it was a private home
the guy built it
was a millionaire
and our own textile town
was the home
of this guy tried to corner
the world market in copper
the woodwork in it was amazing
but by the time I lived there
it was seedy
drunks and all kinds
of deals going on
and who else there but Miss Mulligan
my teacher from junior high
well a druggie's private lab
starts a fire
and I run to get Miss Mulligan
and two punks are there
robbing her apartment
it's like Rome burning
I'm yelling get out of here
the place is on fire
and this lady's my geography teacher
but the lady
doesn't want to leave her home
and the punks and I
are trying to carry her out
when Engine Number Seven
from Stevens Street shows up
we get her out
and the paper's full

of the prodigious efforts
of the fire department
rescuing four recalcitrant residents
but true is we almost got fried
just like the guy
tried to corner copper
in Lowell, Massachusetts

solid state physics

feel free
if you have a question
go ahead and ask it
don't just sit there just thinking
your question foolish
or simpleminded
go right ahead
ask it
perhaps someone else in the class
has the very same question in mind
perhaps someone else in the class
is just as stupid as you are

relativity

in B-326 Doctor Baker
PH 345 3 credits no lab
says
the relativistic force
acting on a particle
is

F mu equals d d tau
open parenthesis
m nought
d x mu
d t
close parenthesis

this force is called the Minkowski force
and Joe Zostek
who sits behind me
says
hurray for the Polak

my landlady's daughter

my landlady was against it
but I was happy to help
her daughter in a graduate education course
in educational testing
I did great
with the Peabody Picture Vocabulary
and terrific in the Wisc-Benet
but the tests got more complex harder
and the tester did not help
the smirk at the wrong answer
the feigned sympathy at the wrong guess
and then she brought out the cards
my landlady was horrified
don't do it don't do it
those cards said awful things about me
at which the daughter rolled her eyes
I was going to do it though
it was the strangest thing
you arrange colors
in your own preference
and then look up the arrangement in a book
to tell you who you are
my landlady's daughter asserted
I don't care who you are
as I could see she memorized my order
I took the book
and looked up the definition
of my psyche
how I was someone took tests

rum drunk

his party trick was lighting up a rum drink and bringing it so
quickly to his mouth that the flames went out as he drank it but
this was with a fraternity punch kind of drink with the proof of
Zapple and when I take him to a party at Celeste's house the drinks
there all top shelf from what she could steal from her dad and the
flames on his rum drink at this party did not go out and while I
am not stating he drank flaming liquid but rather he stopped his
mouth just in time so that the lit liquid went all over his face and
with his thrashing and spilling and yelling and screaming he is
never the kind of person even give a second think about how he
might embarrass a friend or nothing like that I am stating it was
really some party and when I see him now I say you go get your
Thesaurus look up flaming

early morning before the optics final

am I ready for this one?
I am going to ace this for sure
probability one
go head ask me something
all the picayune stuff he likes to ask
every esoteric detail
is up in the memoirs
go head
ask me something
ask me anything
I'm golden this morning
I'm golden

getting so

it's getting so
you can't drive a car
on the streets these days
without having some asshole
run inta ya car
denting it all over
or like
in my case
driving along the highway
and having
a guard rail jump out in front of the car
those fuckers are fast

my brother the helper

by his wife and ex-girlfriend
slut A and slut B
my brother Jimmy had five children
and I asked him to help me move
after all I'd helped him move
way back and he could return the favor
ah no
he can't
and the reason he can't is
my son Greg
had the mumps recently
and Jimmy tells my mother
he doesn't want
to be near us
because he might want
have more children
he thinks catching the mumps
would prevent it
mom says Jimmy
already has too many
he should go give Greg
a great big hug

Lowell poem

you know what
your problem is?
you asked me to go steady
did it kill you doing that?
I'm twenty-eight years old
veryveryvery big deal
I can't wait tell
all my girl friends
from high school
wait let me borrow your cell
at which point
my cellphone
went out the car window
over the railing
of the Aiken Street bridge
and into the waters
of the mighty Merrimack

Maryann

for Maryann Plunkett

how would you like
to stay out of school
a couple of days
she was such a girl
she was so genteel
she just dabbed the stuff
here and there on the arm
and I rubbed
the poison ivy everywhere
I was so smart
I was absent for two weeks of agony
I never had a chance
she went on
to fame and film
and Broadway
and if I look
at a picture of her even now
I break out

glazed

often flying high herself
a pretty girl in my building
loves birds
gives them Irish names
Conor Tim Kevin Bri
so when I saw donut fragments
outside her window on the ground
I thought
she must have been
feeding birds outside
but no another neighbor
one with big eyes big mouth
explained   a boy friend
was trying to attract her attention
by throwing donuts at her window
and I looked up at the window there
all kinds of filling
jam powdered sugar and glaze
on or around the frame
the sill and cross pieces
the glass
the window glasses
you know the panes the panes

golf outing

the river runs through it
and the Vesper is the premier club
in Greater Lowell
doctors judges lawyers
and bail bondsmen golf there
but just like the Vesper
the Tyngsboro Country Club
is on the Merrimack River too
and it was the TCC
for my bachelor party
Matt is my littler brother
he's six four
weighs two ninety-five
my other brother Luke
the older
says Matt's just a veal cutlet
away from three hundred
the bachelor party was small
the two dads and me first
and my two brothers
and Bruno brother-in-law to be
a threesome playing behind
my brothers both hockey players
care nothing about golf
were drinking right away
and they would run up to the ball
on its tee and golf club it like a puck
and really it'd go pretty far
well by the eight ball
Bruno had enough
he walks up to us old guys and asks
can I play with yis
your brothers are going
to throw me in the river
and I look behind

see my brothers chanting Bruno Bruno
with Matt doing swimming gestures
and Luke both hands clasped in front
like he's praying
but then goes into a fake diving motion
as if into a pool or ocean or maybe a river

severed head

there was the A row
B row and so on
Louie Eno and I
were in the other row
when Sister James had pneumonia
and the sub was the principal
the Sister Superior
Vincent Ferrer
who asks the question
what did Marco Polo discover?
right away Louie raises his hand
and he never raises his hand
I am whispering behind him
put your hand down, Lou
too late
yes, Louis, she says
he stands up and says
Marco Polo discovered polo
Sister gets her ruler
this a foot long half inch thick weapon
and whacks him on the top of the head
but the stick lands on its edge
the metal insert into the wood
splits the skin real bad
he bled all over
had to go to hospital for stitches
his mother takes him
out of Saint Michael's
transfers him to the Varnum
I see him much later
and says to him
Lou, why'd y'ever raise your hand?
why say Marco Polo discovered polo?
and Louie goes
he did didn't he?
he goes you know
Mongolian horsemen with a severed head

beautiful day

I never saw the guy before
I never saw him since
but knew him to be
someone said so
Jim Quiglia's older brother
and my first day of high school
he stabbed me in the butt
with a geometry compass
on a stairway
and after school same day
he beat me up in the alleyway
behind Cherry & Webb's
the second day of high school
he beat me up too same place
and the third day
he didn't beat me up
he'd broke his right hand
on a fire escape
someone told me
more than four bones were broken
there are some days
you have to remember
for being so beautiful
of course all forgiven now
water bridge
I wish him peace
and if I see him now
I want to tell you
I would be glad to shake his hand
hard

Blue Dot Sign

she was walking down Bridge Street
to the Blue Dot
to buy a half pound
for Saint Patrick's Day
box of candy
for Sister Vincent Ferrer
she was already in the car
when she told me that
or I wouldn't have offered a ride
in my pink Cadillac
buy a gift for Sister Vincent Ferrer?
not my favorite person
Sister Vincent an Irishman?
you must have to be kidding me
but my passenger
Sister James
asks me
Albert, how did you get
the money for such a nice car?
as if I stole
I stall
it is something like a secret
you have to be discreet
you wouldn't spread this around?
promise you won't tell, Sister
y'have to keep this quiet
as if this is a confessional you know
you won't tell anybody promise right?
so she promises silence
and as she gets out of the car
I says
 Sister, I rob banks
and she starts crossing herself
really really fast
looking up to heaven
after every sign

Lowell Sun "Day to Day"

when I grew up in Lowell
there were immigrant kids at school
but they were Greek or Portygee
and the poorer kids in winter
would wear socks instead of mittens
then as now in the *Lowell Sun*
the police log
is called "Day to Day"
I teach now and
I look at it every day
it has changed ethnically
the two Khmer brothers
students at my school
Sock On and Sock Off
their names weren't exactly those
but oh they were trouble
even in separate rooms
and for sure
they appear in the *Sun* column
regularly
On and Off the teachers called them
teachers can be brutal
the name Flaherty I saw recently
his name rang whistles
this guy the type
the worst kid ever in any teacher's room
so happened was my best friend student
he was arrested at age thirty-two
for an open container violation
the *Sun* even mentioned the brand
Pickwick Light Ale
an obscure high end beverage
quite a distance
from his fourth grade questionnaire
his like then Taylor's Pink Catawba

Taylor's Pink Catawba

the beginning of the school year
Morey School teachers
get quotas so many A students
so many B students and so forth
my teaching the fourth grade
I give out the questionnaires
and the answers
tell a lot about the kids
and it is very helpful
what they like dislike
one boy said he didn't like fathers
that particular kid Flaherty
I was warned about
not one of my A's
oh Flaherty's like
Taylor's Pink Catawba wine
someone like that
I have to relate to
and sure enough
Flaherty and I get along
to the splendid degree
that if another young man
was giving me trouble
Flaherty would give him trouble
I asked him once
Mrs. Gendron said
she had arguments with you
last year, Johnny
why don't you argue with me
he said you look like my auntie
as compliments go
I'll take it

my electronics company

My electronics company use to take apart Japanese televisions in order to bypass international patents and while that sounds sleazy, the place was a class act. There might be some kind of outfit on Route 128 that's not a defense plant but if so, I don't know about it. The one I worked at certainly was and because of that, I was there as a security guard with government clearance for the mandated round-the-clock security. It was a class gig with blue blazers with a pocket with the company coat of arms. Gray pants, white shirt, and navy tie with company emblem tie pin all provided. No weapon though, and I could tell some of my comrades wanted heaters. Once I asked one of the computer scientists Shirley, why does Gerry wait for you to walk to the car parking lot nights. You car pool? Chivalrous he don't impress me as being or should I mind my own business? Shirley was a nice woman, had found a home for George's cat's kittens. Very easy going, she didn't mind my asking that question. She said because he's afraid of the sniper; she even showed me some newspaper clippings in her drawer. Three months before I was hired, a programmer was shot in the head with a deer rifle in the company parking lot on the way to his car; Gerry figures the sniper would have to be very mean to shoot at him when he's walking near Shirley. Oh gees I said. Shirley's telling me was the first I heard of it. It added a little thrill to the night watchman round outside the building. From then on I use to make the fifty minute walk in three seconds.

driving while under the influence
the company pool
foreman
dye house
same guy again
Walter's sore feet
coffee truck
the night the fight with Bill happened
break room
just one B & E
maintenance
forklift driver
desert boots
my youngest that tall
Mill News

2

driving while under the influence

it was three AM and I hit
the blinking yellow light
on the Route Three rotary near Drum Hill
we get out quick
to throw away beer cans
and then I backed up the car a bit
and tried to go forward
but the car wouldn't go forward
so I backed up around the rotary
into a gas station
I figured I could put my car
in the row of cars already there
and nobody would notice right?
I get out and hide behind but
by this time I can see the flashing lights
and it was really something
the police cruiser goes around the rotary
takes the exit I took
and comes right to me
I was alone all my friends split
and they get me for leaving the scene
driving under the influence
and being a minor in possession
all kinds of stuff right?
I asked the guy found me
how'd you catch me?
he said he followed the leaking radiator
it leaked after the crash right?
fifty million dumb cops in the world
and this guy
has to be a genius

the company pool

ya want ta be in our pool?
I was gonna axk ya sooner
but I didn't know
if ya wanted ta
I'll show ya how it works
ya pay a dollar an a quarter
ya givit ta me
but you'll haf ta start next week
the dollar goes inta the home run pool
and ya don't haf ta pay the quarter
unless if ya want ta
we use *The Record*
and we check out the runs column
on the sports page
not that this paper's always right
in fact it usually aint right
but this is the paper we use anyway
ya gotta use something ta go by
the team with the most runs
at the end a the week
the guy with that team wins the pool
the quarter is for the thirteen run pool
if ya team gets exactly thirteen runs
ya win that
that don't happen too often
Alfred over there
made thirty bucks last week winning that
so if ya want ta
ya can be in that one too
ya see we pick the team from this can
every week
so one guy don't get stuck
with the same shitty team
the tricky thing is
that the week for the pool

starts on Thursday and for the paper
it starts on Monday
so we just carry it over
y'understand this?

foreman

Walter walked over to Alfred
and asked him
to mix up the soap
when he got the chance
and Alfred said
sure he'd do it
when he got the chance
but he never did it
so Walter walked over to Ronald
and said
Ron, why don't ya make the soap up
when ya through what ya doin
and Ronald said
fuck you, Walter
of course
Ronald went and mixed up the soap
when he got the chance
Walter noticed it too
they didn't make Walter
the boss for nothing

dye house

the same guy use to shine his shoes
with the cloth
that was goin into the kettle
while the kettle was heatin up
one day it looped round his foot
lifted him right up
his foot went through the eye
and got stuck in the rollers
with five hundred pounds pressure
the water wasn't hot
and his leg didn't go through the rollers
but still he hurt his foot
his arms his ribs his head
he was out of work two months
how'd it happen?
gee I don't know
must've stepped on it somehow
he gets back out of the hospital
and comes back to work
he's loadin kettle three
when Walter and me
come round the corner
we see him tryin the same thing again
shinin his shoes with the movin cloth
Walter says to him
out the fuckin door
and real quick
he was on the outside lookin in

same guy again

the same fuckin guy
before they had the caustic tank
they used to have flakes
and you had to mix the stuff
you had to be careful too
fuckin stuff would burn
this new guy
he throws a bucket of the stuff
into the kettle
it splashes back
his ass was on fire
runnin all over the dye house
Walter chasin after him
it was Alfred and me caught him
and Walter helped us
throw him in the soap barrel
same fuckin guy
was gonna bring home
industrial peroxide
for his wife to dye her hair
Walter caught him then
just in time
of course right now
that guy is on the outside
lookin in

Walter's sore feet

I used to feel like
picking up my fuckin feet
putting em in my fuckin pocket
and walking on my fuckin knees
so now I do what my chiropractor says
I spend ten minutes every night
rolling my feet each one
over a bunch of golf balls
in a shoe box
it's been helping me a lot
and once you get used to it
it's no trouble at all
since I started using two shoe boxes
it's cut the time in half

coffee truck

the coffee truck once ran out
of Tahitian Treat at the mill
so for a long time I used to get Wink
and the coffee truck guy
told me a story
he said the mending room girls
always use to get
Halfnhalf with their lunch
then for a long time
he couldn't get Halfnhalf
only Polynesian Punch
and when he got Halfnhalf back
they wouldn't touch it
they was so use
to getting Polynesian Punch
so when the guy got back
Tahitian Treat
he thought I wasn't gonna touch it either
but I went right back
to getting Tahitian Treat
no more Wink for me after that
I fooled the guy
and he was surprised too

the night the fight with Bill happened

that same night
after they beat up Bill
they came back
don't you know
shithead was mad
because Ray broke up the fight
and so he brought back his gang
a bunch of them
clean out the mill
that's what he said
I'm gonna clean out the mill
the dye house
and the second shift upstairs
hears all the noise
and run down and
those assholes left quick enough
through the doors
out the windows
only new guy got hurt
one of the dips
lost a shoe at the window
rushing out of it
sixteen year old kids
gonna beat up grown men
gonna clean out the mill

break room

coffee break yesterday
one of the office girls
stops by the Coke machine
and she is wearing a dress
and looks really fine
something like wrapped
in a pink towel
with sparkling tights
and Mo is looking at her
all the time she is there
and she's leaving
he goes
        hey, you
and she turns around
and I'm hiding my head in my arm
for what he's about to say
and he goes
           what a pretty dress

just one B & E

once they git me for sniffin glue
which almost don't count
cuz like it was nothin
and then there was just one B & E
was all they git me for
just one
but no more because I'm a good boy now
I promised my mother
but like if anybody
needs any power tools
lemme know by
before this weekend
cuz like as far's my mother's concerned
good boys are ones don't get caught

maintenance

we don't got enough to do around here
maintenance can't lift barrels
we gotta lift the barrels
four hundred fifty pound barrels
I bring in a barrel
and then go back to maintenance
and there's
fuckin Roger back there doin nothin
fuckin John back there doin nothin
fuckin Willsie back there doin nothin
Willsie's eighty years old
I'm not axin him bring in no barrel
but what about fuckin Roger or John
you don't axk an eighty year old man
to bring in no fuckin barrel

forklift driver

the forklift driver
fucked up the elevator again
he tried to drive the forklift in it
when the door was closed
this is the third day in a row
something like that happened
I'd say to him
don't even bother ta punch out
just leave
it'd be worth the week's pay or so
just to get rid of him
do you know how important
that fuckin elevator is?
Lou is yellin all over for yarn
because he can't get it
and this is holding up the knitting room
napping room and the whole place
gonna be backed up now
they tell me Lou
is pissin and moanin up there
like he was pissin razor blades

desert boots

I was calling from the police station
at four AM and I'm sayin to myself
let it be dad answers the phone
let it be dad don't let ma answer
and so after thirty rings
my mother answers the phone
I say real nice and quiet
ma, could I speak to dad please?
she must have known from my tone
I was not being wiseass
that something was wrong
she says OK and I tell my father
what happens how I am at the station
for drunk driving leaving scene
a minor in possession
and how the car is all messed up
so please come and get me, dad
I tell all the story
not even guessing
my mother's on the extension
I get home and finally crash on the bed
with my clothes on
just takin off my desert boots
hanging them up on the floor
while I'm sleepin
who goes out and checks out
my latest crash scene
but mom and dad
they were impressed with the damage
and as soon as they return home
here I am in a deep sleep
and I slowly begin to notice
someone pounding on my face
with a pair of desert boots
I am yellin ma, ma

help me help me
but I was all mixed up
it was ma hitting me
and my father stops her
those boots were really heavy
and really hurt
and I started acting careful after that
wearin sneakers from then on

my youngest that tall

they kept on sending him home last year
the fuckin kid was always actin up
so last summer
all through the summer
they were buildin a new school
near the house
and we kept on
pointing out the fuckin thing
tryin to get the kid interested you know
see the school they're buildin for you
that sure is a nice lookin school
so the wife takes him
to the second grade to register
and the kid looks around him
and right in front of the teacher
he says to her
I aint stayin in this fuckin place
my wife said she felt about this fuckin tall

Mill News

Congratulations for Joe Bonmarche (knitting) on his retirement. Don't work too hard with the golf balls, Joe.

Best wishes for Magloire (Muggy) Houle with his new job at Crane Knitting.

Best wishes for Gerard Boisvert (drier room) with his new job plans.

Good luck for Ronald Beausoleil (dye house) in his criminal justice studies and his work at Dino's Oldsmobile and Shell Station.

CONGRATULATIONS

Congratulations for Florette Boisvert's (knitting) citation from the Captain of the Queen Anna Maria for her rendition of "La Vie en Rose."

TERMINATIONS

We hope that the two former employees of maintenance and the stockroom, recently incarcerated at the Billerica Jail, will once again become constructive citizens after appropriate rehabilitation.

the company physical combat proficiency test average

the company average'd be higher
but Ramos there
he went inta the mile run
with a near four hunnerd
burnt smoke fer the first three laps
an then he got sick
an a committee group sergeant there
another Puerto Rican fella
told him ta quit ta leave
an so he got a zeero on the whole test
an that brought the company average
down a point an a half
in my opinion Ramos got fucked
he could a lowcrawled his ass
the rest a the way
an still a got a four fifty
if I'd a seed that sergeant there
I'm not ascairt a nobody
I'd a beat the shit out a him
but don't feel bad, Ramos
what's done is did
that's all right, son
ya git another chance tomorrer
though that don't help
the company average none

to Sergeant Rock

gentlemen
one year over there
an you'll age ten
am I exaggeratin, Sergeant Rock?
you ask Sergeant Rock
if I'm exaggeratin
Sergeant Rock was in the army
since the day he was born
he was in the war of the babies

main gate

the bus driver is furious
but I am bored
I stop the bus
and avoid the rolling Pepsi can
I speak with a command voice
ID cards and passes please
one troop shows me an ID
but does not have a pass
my sergeant gave me a two ten verbal pass
and I got to give you this speech I says
you are under apprehension
for attempted AWOL
I must advise you of your rights
under Article Thirty-one
of the Uniform Code of Military Justice
you have the right to remain silent
and anything you say may be used
against you at trial by courts martial
you have a right to an attorney
either civilian or military
however a civilian attorney
would be at your own expense
you have to come with me now
the girl with him begins to cry
what am I going to do?
and I say
I have no jurisdiction over you, miss
about a week later I figure out
she's talking to the troop and not to me
the willie had slash scars on his wrists
oh I catch on so quick

riot control school

I thought maybe
he's a guy
that puts himself
in other people's stories
ya know samesame Walter Mitty
so maybe it happened
to someone else and
he only stole the story
men
gentlemen
I been in three world wars
World War Two
Korea
and Santo Domingo
we looked at each other then
Santo Domingo?
and let me tell you
gentlemen
that was a war
with a capital doubleyou
they threw everything at us
I was point man
in a wedge formation
and I got hit on the head
with a Coke bottle Molotov cocktail
but
I
kept
on
going
and everyone thought that
this was all bullshit
but I thought maybe
that was what
went wrong with his head

Outpatient Clinic, General Wood Hospital

the provost marshal
would send a patrol car to OPC
for lots of things
animal bites
traffic accidents
wife beatings
the most common
but there were suicides too
and attempts at it
poisonings say
and with a force for a giraffe's neck
Nurse Jones would push a tube
down a willie's throat
she was the nicest nurse lieutenant
at the General Leonard Wood Army Hospital
but she said she spends
too much time and effort
trying to make people live
to have any sympathy for a dink
attempting the opposite
the real ones never made it
deep razor cuts
gunshots or hangings
but there were always
some overdoses of aspirin
one willie poisoned himself
drinking Brasso
and at the company orderly room
where we picked him up
he's in agony
blaming the sergeants
for not calling the police sooner
but at the OPC
as they're ready
to pump out his stomach

he is asking Nurse Jones
if officers can date enlisteds
Lieutenant Jones did not answer
but with an ill humor
she pumped out his guts
she had fun with that one

Mastrantonio and the rhinoceros beetle

Mastrantonio looks
and points to something on the ground
and yells
booo man hey wowww
look at that will ya?
that's a rhinoceros beetle
but I never seen one that big
I never seen one that ugly
it looks like Markham
when he wakes up in the morning
sheeit it looks like Markham
anytime a day
don't get too close
that can really hurt ya
gimme a pencil
gimme something it can latch onto
hey, Markham, gimme ya finger
and Markham gives Mastrantonio a finger

Paco

when I was radio operator
I sent Paco
on a larceny
of personal property
at Headquarters
Special Troops
Paco calls back on the radio
ten-twenty that last ten-twenty-four
disregard ignore shitcan that last assignment
the dude
found his dust

Manwarring's defenestration

the parolees just breached
some of them
but the maximum custody barracks
the box actually rioted
most of the guards there
made it to the turnkey
at the sally port gate
but Diogati and Manwarring
were guarding the upstairs
and did not wake up in time
from sleeping on empty bunks
so with the sound of breaking glass
and yelling and screaming
they the prisoners
threw Manwarring and Diogati
out the second story windows
Diogati says
that he did not scream
like Manwarring
when they was throwed
out the window
but best be advised
you better believe
he yelled like hell

Serious Incident Report:
Maltreatment of Trainee

this here sergeant's
shit is flaky
I aint even bullshittin
seven willies from another unit
seen him kick
this trainee
in the balls
an this trainee is hurtin
I aint even bulljivin
all the doctor can do
is put ice down there
doctor says
the dude'll
be sterile
in at least the left nut
doctor says
his balls is
flat as a pancake

sierra tango

Wild Irish Rose Wine
quart bottle half full
was found unsecured
in subject's vehicle
subject became belligerent
and directed profanity
towards Mike Papa Armen
such reprehensible conduct
merited subject ride
to provost marshal's office
where subject was cited
and released to unit
on Department of Defense
Form six two niner
subject's vehicle was secured
at scene by mike papas
did they ever whip
his sorry ass
lots of stick time there

guardmount speech

you guards in fifty
listen up
there's a man there Ankabrant
someone puts the kibosh to
ever night
Anklebrink's at the sally port
right now behind ya
they set his bunk on fire tonight
yesterday they kiboshed him on the head
an threw water on him
an the day fore that
they hid his clothes
under the barracks
so you guys
watch Ankenbrink's bunk
it's the first un
on the left downstairs
the duty officer suggest
when you fall asleep
you all fall asleep
in a circle around Ankenbrank's bunk
that was the duty officer bein funny

one lifeguard, rescued

Hernandez lucked out
and along with Reyes
had to check out the incident
at the WAC shack
the middle of the night
the middle of the summer
girls in skimpy PJs
with shovels and rakes
and even a grass scythe
a willie got caught
climbing up the fire escape
and the Spanish Soul patrol
had to rescue his ass from all the girls
dude claimed he was the lifeguard

gift rabbit

white hat patrol at Fort Wood
Roosevelt's driving on base
through the NCO family quarters
we call these places hovels outside he says
he sees a white rabbit on the road
subject creature obviously a parolee
from some Easter gift cage
Roosevelt drives out of his way
to hit the rabbit
kills it with the Chevy Two
military police cruiser
says to me
that's what it gets
f'bein white
you know you can tell right away
when someone doesn't like animals

churchkey

I hung out with Emanuel Klawere
and that's why
Irish name aside
the Executive Sergeant Boddoms
had both of us on his list
he thought I was Jewish
once we needed a bottle opener
and Emanuel goes
into a liquor store off base
and asks for a synagogue key
and I have a theory about this
there are so many Baptists
in Missouri that when they go for beer
they too embarrassed
to ask for a churchkey
they ask for a synagogue key instead
and the strict Baptists you know
they don't gamble either
you can bet on it

ten-ten the area

some women
would get lonely
with husbands away
and call in frivolous
made up complaints
Bill the radio man calls us
a prowler
purportedly
at the married NCO housing area
and Roes was driving the cruiser
and he was familiar with the address
and he really hauls
to the house
on Beauregard Street
streets there all named for rebels
we get to the house
but the patrol supervisor
was there before Roes
the patrol supervisor
did not want our help
and says to us
I'll take care of this, Ross
you an Klawere beat feet
ten-ten the area

my brother-in-law and me

my brother-in-law and me
we came back from work
with a case of beer
this was after working overtime
and we walk into the door
and I see my wife
sitting on the couch
with her bra and panties on
and this guy I never seen before
is standing in front of the TV
in his shorts
turning it on
I say to my brother-in-law
let's get out of here
and we walked out
we drunk the beer at his house

the bear

the carnival on base had a trained bear
moth-eaten ancient
the thing kills its trainer
swipes the trainer good on the neck
and breaks something vital
though there was not much blood
no claws on the bear
no teeth for that matter
we could not find the dog officer
and Lieutenant Davis bravely shot the bear
so the medics could go in the cage
get the trainer
next day someone steps on a puppy
at the carnival
the animal some poor kind of hound
a Lowell retriever
a prize at one of the games
and the poor thing was hurting
we again could not find the dog officer
Roes suggested we call for Lieutenant Davis
him the dog officer ipso facto aint he?

Davis and the lion

the brigade mascot breached
escaped from its half garage sized pen
I thought we'd never find it
although all cars were ordered to search
except the dog catcher
we could never find him
oh we'll never find
that catamount
I am thinking
when I hear
over the radio
close that fuckin door
we did find it
hiding in a corner
of the yard of the base library
now Sergeant Tenewicz
said his dogs would tree it
but there it is
in the midst of two foot tall shrubs
we try to herd it
into a portable cleaning cage
the lion looks at the cage
and looks at Tenewicz' beagles
and jumps for Lieutenant Davis
Davis shoots it on the fly
with a forty-five no less
and kilt it
even the dogs were impressed
they stopped barking
started whimpering
and then were quiet
and animals all over Missouri
were ascairt of Davis then on
lions and beagles and bears

crash shatter

people off duty left early
so as not to be called for stand-by
call them stand-by evaders around here
but last night
when those individuals got back
after movies
or NCO clubs
that's when it started
the prisoners breaking windows
everyone was called
they gave the cooks and clerks
MP helmets and clubs
to bust heads
they had us rushing
from barracks to barracks
with a firehose and so
a dozen twenty or so pees
no more maybe forty
and prisoners from other barracks
each yard ringed with its own wire
were cheering
as prisoners from one barracks
were chased and clubbed
outside in their underwear
the firehose never turned on
once they yelled turn it on
and nothing happened
and another time they yell turn it on
and then a louder wait a minute
and maybe a quart of water dribbles out
and a prisoner walks by saying
everyone crazy here
someone have to mop that up

the hogtieing of Montgomery

Canney had a straw color Villa mustache
reddish blond hair and beer gut
coaches told him lift weights and drink beer
concussed in a football game
he refused to play again
and the college took away his scholarship
the draft happens and he has
real nice words to say about football coaches
with the loudest voice in the world
at the riot Canney yells
they got you here, Case?
even white hats here?
aint this a hassle?
he points to a prisoner in front of the rioters
subject lighting matches one at a time
see him? that's Montgomery
one strong little dude
we brought him back from the hospital
little dude got his arms free
and biff
right between the eyes ouuhh
I saw little stars like in cartoons
only more plentiful you know
watch now we gonna put him
in a non-transient condition

Warren in the rye

Grant goes
I have to tell you, Sergeant
that your son Worn
mouthed off
he was really a wise ass
and we had to slap him
around a bit
we found this book on Worn
you might want to watch out
for what he reads
so he don't get alienated
with everyday life

frisk

drunk against the wall
at the provost marshal's
Roes kicks the guy's left foot further apart
I kick the right foot
so he's really leaning against the wall
four five feet easy away from the base
like a hypotenuse
but the drunk is saying horrible things
eff this eff that and worse
Roes should have kept quiet
but instead says to him
who taught you how to talk that nice?
guy replies
your mother and his sister
Harry and I didn't say a word to him
we just looked at each other
and then kicked
the drunk's feet away from the wall
his face fell nose first
flat on the concrete
his neck actually cracks and snaps up
and I would not have cared more less
it was Harry's fault anyway
he should a kept quiet
I don't even have a sister

463rd Military Police Company, Escort Guard

the mess steward for the 463rd
famous fort wide
for being a major prick
shoving round the trainees
and then the stockade prisoners
but then he got sent to the 463rd
and he starts bossing MPs around
these guys not all new guys
these people permanent party
some of them returnees from the big country
and the mess steward
has just re-upped
bought hisself an olive drab Duster
with his bonus money
for four more years of his life
he finishes work one day
and goes to his new car
the keyholes all punched in
all hubcaps gone AWOL
tires punctured
upholstery slashed
and doused with eggs
sugar in the gas tank
sardines in every crevice
all windows shattered
except for the windshield
where was etched the word
poached

Cookies out of humor

Cookies ran away actually AWOL
with a sixteen year old daughter
of some NCO and
when he gets back they fine him
give him extra duty
and moreover
the sweet young girl
he forced to marry
turns into instant bitch
and morningtimes
not Cookies' best for good humor
to begin with
so there's Wesley
when Cookies asks him
how he wants his eggs
Wesley says poached
and Cookies goes nuts
waddles around the corner
and is pushing Wesley
with his chest
and Wesley's yelling scairt
I aint running from you, Cookies
I aint running from you
and thing is
Cookies still has a huge fork in his hand
well what to do
I get in between and start shouting
don't hit my brother, Cookies
else I bleed all over yis
Cookies starts laughing at this
later Wesley is pissed
I could have taken him, man
but you got in the way

whichwaydidhego
whichwaydidhego

one barracks
filled with OJT people
military police in training
one of the trainees from there
runs into our barracks once
I'm the only one there
he yells at me
where's Blankenship?
I says I don't know who Blankenship is
I didn't ask you that
I asked you where is he?
I pointed out the barracks
the far door
and off he went
mad as a lark at dusk
at Blankenship

last patrol

them two always arguing
arguing at MP school
and then later when
they permanent party personnel
they always arguing at Fort Wood
the southerner the northerner
now they both get orders
from the adjutant general levy section
the very same day
the specialist asks
is there anything
that would keep you
from going to Vietnam?
so both of them
are so slick
think they can fight the system
that they can gainget a favor out of it
both of them go to the provost marshal
and ask in behalves of old times
if they last day there
can be on patrol together
not with a jeep
like those losers in the 463rd
Escort Guard Company
but with an MP Chevy Two cruiser
in which they can wear white hats
now you know what happens
all the time on patrol
they argue who is senior man
they have such a wonderful time
that's what they call beat the system
if you a couple of dumb shits

4

learning

I like learning useless things
like Latin
I really enjoyed Latin
Caesar and the Gallic Wars
enjoyed his fighting
the Helvetians and Germans
and Gauls
I enjoyed Vietnamese too
the language
its five intonations
its no conjugations
a good language to learn
Vietnam is divided in
three parts too
it makes me wonder
who will write their book

welcome

Welcome to building 950
Gateway to the Pacific
Group leaders report to shipping office
No females allowed

gentlemen
attendance at these mandatory formations
is of primary concern
with us group leaders
I want to see all you smiling faces
with me in the big country
also we'll be flying on an airplane
with two young ladies, gentlemen
with two stewardesses
ya American soldiers
an grown-up men
construct yaselves accordingly

a bummer

we were going single file
through his rice paddies
and the farmer
started hitting the lead track
with a rake
he wouldn't stop
the TC went to talk to him
and the farmer
tried to hit him too
so the tracks went sideways
side by side
through the guy's fields
instead of single file
Hard On, Proud Mary
Bummer, Wallace, Rosemary's Baby
The Rutgers Road Runner
and
Go Get Em—Done Got Em
went side by side
through the fields
  if you have a farm in Vietnam
and a house in hell
sell the farm
and go home

message in the public interest

happiness
is when
the person
you hate most
in the whole world
gets the clap
for the third time
so if you think
you
have VD
the burning
the dripping
sensation
see the medic
at your aid station
right now
and
stay out
of the Yucatan rain forest
this is the
Armed Forces Vietnam Network
the best of music
here
from everywhere
from Monkey Mountain

seven letters for Harmon

Harmon, listen up
you aint here yet, troop?
I got seven letters today, Harmon
seven whole letters
you got no letters today
zeero letters yesterday
and zeero letters the day fore that
you don't know seven people
who might want to write to you
let alone seven people
who even know how to write
hey, troop
quit it, Harmon
keep your grubby hands
off my letters

dog cemetery

seeing the man praying at the dog cemetery
Bagley yells out
you wanta believe in dog heaven, man
you go right ahead, man
knock yaself out, man
and we drive closer
and the guy looks up and he is an officer
in reality the officer in charge
of the scout dog platoon
his look at ya just regular
would freeze steel to boiling
and this time he is really mad
and Bagley drives
that jeep away really fast
but this is an MP jeep
has 23rd MP Company all over it
even covering the spare tire in back
and now which MP d'you think
did the lieutenant blame for this?
every single one
he'd drive by in his jeep
at the MP bunker at the main gate
and look at you
you was worth absolutely nothing
if you didn't believe in dog heaven

shotgun ride

Lonnie Kingman is telling you
get on you steel pot
bandolier
MP brassard
M-16 and flak jacket
MP brassard I say that twice
so as you can ride shotgun
oh no you don't sit with the driver
Lonnie Kingman do that
Lonnie Kingman shotgun rider one
you shotgun rider two
we did that before
Lonnie Kingman himself
just one rifle up front
half the prisoners
leave out the back
before Lonnie
figure out beans
when the bag was opened

the death truck

yellow flags with three red stripes
flowers
wreaths
banners
and
smell
mark
the death truck
I
never
seen
one
stop

shotgun rider two

Lonnie tells me
the prisoner run
don't mean nothing
there's beaucoup
but most of them civilian detainees
just a couple of armed draft dodgers
this time again
I am in the back
of the three quarter ton
but this time
there's a lot of prisoners
I am at the very back
on one of the side benches
right arm holding the rifle
stock on thigh
and the left arm
holding on to the railing
the prisoner to my left
puts his right arm around my shoulders
to prevent me from falling off
no no can't do that
khong the duoc khong the duoc
I tell Bagley about it later big mistake
asked him
why didn't the prisoner
just push me off the truck and book?
and Bagley thinks says you know
half these gooks are queer

John on jeep hood

yoyoyoyo sound of duckherds
the mud flats of Sam Tin
the barefoot children
two feet tall
with twenty foot bamboo poles
herding livestock
occasionally one kid
one water buffalo
but mostly ducks
twenty thirty a hundred
yoyoyoyo
John sits on the jeep hood
waving at children left right
pointing benignly
hello hello looking good, kid
looking good like that shirt
or authoritatively
best be advised
look sharp, dudes
where's your hat?
troop, why aint you in school?
why aren't your boots laced?
not gonna get nowhere, Joe
not tying your shoes
hey
you know where I can find some ducks?
you ask
why one kid can herd fifty animals
each with its own mind albeit dim?
why those animals
don't go every which way?
I answer
thing is
you just herd the chief duck
and all the stupid buddies follow
yoyoyoyo

John and the Kalashnikov

John brings one over once
to my area of the hooch
to ostensibly
show me his black market purchase
a genuine AK-47
but the visit real reason really?
he heard I got a big package
from my mother's friend
who made the world's best brownies
wrapped individually in aluminum foil
and then the small foil package
wrapped in Saran Wrap
hey uh buddy, he says very subtle
look at this rifle and by the way
you get a package today?
OK this is the photo of John John
holding the AK-47 sideways
the banana clip
thirty-six bullet capacity
is very visible
but look close at JJ's face
less visible
the outline of six seven reddish
sorts of irregular circles
what a child would draw for circles
JJ had ringworm on his face
Doctor Medina
First of the Fourteenth aid station
prescribed Tinactin
told him
your towels should be washed regularly
unless you are a total idiot

sniper

the M-79 blooker grenade launcher
the Rugers that recon units carried
Valentine's Spanish Star pistol
some really different arms around
I picked up a hitchhiker once
a sniper
and he looked like hell
capable though
an Asian-American
the only one I see in our army
an M-16 with built-on silencer
brass tacks on the stock
your kills? I ask
he goes no
I received this
from my predecessor
they might be kills
but they are not my kills
what else would they be?
I have to say it impresses
the hell out of the natives
I says
I suppose you call it a nickname
Betsy or something
something like that
im he says
hip I say a double metaphor
calling a rifle silence in Vietnamese
and that's what it does to people
and the rifle itself has a silencer
no he says *im* he says
I'm telling you to keep quiet

raiding a whorehouse

the jeep stops and then the three quarter ton and I notice the left lace of my jungle boot untied but I hear shots oh fuck me dead and so I run into the hooch *sin thay xe jip* I yell to Hieu I run through several rooms where there are only children and then down a hallway nobody there then out the back door an American behind the door are you an American? I ask real smart he's twice my size he might be a dink drop what's in your hands he has nothing hands against the wall frisk him nothing Clock the honcho asks any others? I don't know I stopped when I found him more shots further back ruffpuffs show up with two Americans scared beaucoups tell em stop shooting tell em stop shooting in front of the hooch Hieu is still watching the jeep we gotta frisk em, Clock oh yeah I got a forty-five in my belt in front oh yeah thanks for telling me into the three quarter ton jeep goes first the three quarter ton stalls Clock, stop the jeep stop the jeep Clock doesn't hear us at all all right help me push the jeep goes on without us John begins his let-us-let-them-go act the youngest interpreter Giang says the ruffpuffs will never work with us again if we let them go Giang doesn't let us forget he was in the field wears a Marine field cap Giang hard ass with American prisoners the prisoners and Giang and I all start pushing the three quarter ton we get tired and have to rest in front of the house of Miss Huynh Thi who saw us she wears short shorts to bed she tells me I would not know otherwise no *gai diem* her she says later she saw me pushing the three quarter ton you push truck funny hell but I did not see her at the time back at the provost marshal's the big guy who was shivering behind the door he acts hard core I work for the Army Post Office he says what's ya name? and then reads my shirt nametag and says I gonna remember that I says knock yaself out he says y'aint gonna get any mail from now on I says step outside say that? he says oh no just don't spect any mail from now on, Turnwald it's Turnwald's shirt I am wearing see Turnwald left in country three months before ETS freedom bird back to the world I laugh at hard core and notice my shoelace is still untied but nothing trips up John P. Fogerty himself or his mail you know what I mean you know I am saying what I am saying

deploy deploy

the LZ has a middle of the night drill
and the BTOC squad deploys
quick as hell
we sky there less than a minute
and this officer walks around
asks if we got our flak jacket
that's evident eh?
and then he asks
how much ammo you got?
I didn't even have a clip
a real pisser for a drill even?
April Fool's Day they hit us real
and piss burner goes around again
right to the same hole
I'm hiding in
ready for him this time
one hundred seventy-one bullets, sir
nineteen per clip
eight clips in the bandolier
he's says that's not a hundred seventy-one
I says then and one clip in the rifle, sir
locked and loaded, sir
some people you know
they kick at a hanging

the LZ Gator body collector

see
her back is arched
like something's under it
that's why I thought
it was booby trapped
but it's not
it just must have been
over this rock here
and somebody moved it
after corpus morta stiffened it
I didn't know it was
a woman at first
I couldn't tell
but then I grabbed
down there
it's a woman or was
it's all right
I didn't mind
I had gloves on then

on death

school children walk by
some stare
some keep on walking
some adults stare too
with handkerchiefs
over their nose
a woman
sits on the pavement
beside
wails
and pounds her fists
on pavement
flies all over
it like made of wax
no jaw
intestines poured
out of the stomach
the penis in the air
  it won't matter then to me but now
I don't want in death to be a
public obscenity like this

officers club

Albert drives the jeep
by the main gate
with Stanley in back
her eyes red and damp
cheeks wet
but she is not crying just then
she's just looking at me
waiting for me to say something mean
I just log Albert's name and Stanley's name
and the jeep number
on the clipboard list
and Albert goes
I gotta drive Stanley home
the officers club
don't want Stanley there
no way no how
Stanley says nothing
and I was thinking
of a y'all shuddup, Albert
and then thought that
Stanley's gravelly laugh
likely too much
for the serious drunks
I'd told her not to go there
a nasty place
on a hill with a near constant mild breeze
leather bar stools
and picture windows
overlooking the South China Sea
chromed AK-47s under glass
and officers there
blood on every groping paw

poem for Mary Tyler Moore

day before the theater blew up
the movie there was so bad
was never released in the States
title *What's So Bad About Feeling Good?*
it has a bird from South America
spreading a virus through the USA
and the virus makes people nice
to each other and good natured in general
and before everyone knows it
tobacco sales plummet
and the tobacco industry
goes up in a smoky fog
through this insidious affliction
and firearms companies go bankrupt
and the whiskey
companies can't sell their popskull rotgut
and Wall Street buys off the government
hard to believe
to fight this plague
while the contagion spreads to other nations
and the Pentagon is furious
with the virulence
of this condition
all these vital institutions
band together
to kill the bird
whereupon the heroine Norma Normal
who bought the original bird
finds an egg on the pillow
and there is hope again
in the world of this crummy movie
and the next day
the theater went up
two separate explosive charges
one to kill the audience
and the other to kill the people
taking care of the audience

Victor

my Victor November friend and me
his arm would not move
would not go around
so my arm is around his shoulder
they suggested
I close my eyes to look like his
and then they backed up the jeep
to take the picture looking down
and that is why the ground
is the actual background for the picture
except for that and the flies
the picture they took
makes both of us look alive

downtown residential An Tan

a child five six years
walks up to me
and shrieks *may gio ruoui?*
I just look at him
he screams *may gio ruoui?*
he's asking me what time is it
I look at my watch
and while I can tell time thank you
I have trouble with the thirty-five past two
in my Vietnamese
the child has trouble too
reading the dial on my wrist
he just slips the watch off and away
and books into the crowd
my Seiko never more seen
big joke of Albert thereafter
asking me what time it is
he don't know
because he don't have no watch
he says I should have known better
stopping the jeep
in that Catholic neighborhood again

Sergeant Le's watch

No Neck walks over
with the gook lieutenant
in charge of interpreters
Sergeant Le you know him
die
him father give him watch
give him ask plee who take watch?
father want him back you know
I said I knew the medics
at the aid station
the First of the Fourteenth Artillery
and I said
while I couldn't promise
I would try to find the watch
I lied

Cenerizio's service

the only time all of us together
the platoon together
I recall wondering
if John's night shift
from the cage would show
they do every single richard
and National Policeman Hieu
and the ARVN QC Hau
National Police Highway Patrolman Long
Interpreter Sergeants Tuats, Son, and Giang
from intelligence
and company at Chu Lai
sends a dozen bodies
to man the gate
the provost marshal's office
the north south patrols
the monkey house
Crazy Rusty relieves me
at the gate
I thank him
de nada he says
at the chapel
all there to hear
Father Bykowski's mass
all his parishioners
there for the combat zone confession
bread and wine
for the unit and attached
except for the dead Cenerizio
and Interpreter Sergeant Le
killed in the same bunker
the same night
same hour same minute
maybe not the same second
but you know it was close very close

personal effects

typed
page four of four
bottle, plastic, orange malaria pills, one
bottle, plastic, white malaria pills, one
jungle wallet, Americal Division emblem, one
finger nail clippers, one
string of beads, plastic, multi-colored, two

photoposter, 2' by 3', girl in white bathing suit
inscribed, "all my love, Mindy how do I look, Greg?", one

written
on diagonal line across page
nothing more follows

Bagley removes a thought

Bagley dumped on Antonio
one particular time
Bagley sees Antonio
sitting leaning forward
and moving his skull
in something of a circle
shaking his head
and Bagley asks him
why? he says
I am removing a thought
and so Bagley scoffs and disparages
so this is the fucking irony
later after Cenerizio is killed
I see Bagley
at the provost marshal's
and he's sitting on the backsteps
leaning forward
turning his head sideways
hitting the ear opposite
the ground
with his hand
slapping himself hard
and you know
I knew exactly what
he wasn't thinking of

pentagon

in country the My Lai tragedy
occurred before my time
and the lesser known Seymour Hersh story
on Ky Chanh, Quang Tin Province
was before my time as well
but my patrol route
on Highway One
was through Ky Chanh
and I remember once near Ky Chanh
seeing children play with a stick and ball
with what looked like a pitcher's mound
and a home plate
and then there were four bases
now I wish I had stopped
taught them something about the game
but that would mean time travel
you can't get there from now

Cap Saint-Jacques

there
over a thousand soldiers
swam for the American warship
he and ten others
reached the vessel
he remembers Captain Bagley well
and Sergeant Dutch
and Casey also
but Casey's rank
he does not recall
his oldest son is a cab driver
which is a very good job
for the tourists
he is no longer a policeman
now he is a farmer
and because
there is no trade embargo currently
he wonders if his brother Casey
would be able to invest in his farm

5

She

imaginary poison dart pipe
to his mouth
he makes the sound *phyyyt*
she walks by so dressed
or he moves his hands
one thumb extended
points towards her
and the other draws back
an imaginary elastic band
he whispers the word *zeeeng*
or she slides by styling
and he extends one arm
hand in a fist
and with two fingers
of the other hand
pulls a mythical arrow
from a like quiver
draws back a bow string
and mumbles *twunnnk*
you see he saw her talking to the Bopper
laughing with the Bopper
like she actually enjoyed
the company of the Bopper
he thinks she's on his list now
he don't know it
really it's the other way around

you stink as a boss

Bopper goes we've all done so well
I want to congratulate you all
and Robin goes
can we have an extra hour for lunch?
he goes no
and then she minces her words
says you stink as a boss
and he goes
you can have forty-five minutes
Robin asks extra?
no fifteen minutes on top
of your authorized half-hour
everybody but Robin
 and Robin just smiles
whispers to me
he just cut my regular lunch time
I usually take by thirty minutes
she adds
oh he's gonna hurt
and he's gonna like it

summer sizzler outfit

Bopper's secretarial selection
picked by his wife
selection turns out to be Agnes
Agnes tells me how
that Cindi now
brings on the coffee and donuts
to the Bopper every morning
she stops at the microwave to warm it
because the Bopper likes it hot
donuts plural is right
three of them
confectioner's sugar all over
her fire engine red dress
but Agnes says the red jam
doesn't show on the red
like it used to
on the spaceship silver ensemble

Mister Ahern

much as a fish
was a Christian symbol
it is also a death threat
and Ahern was so horribly upset
when the smell led his red nose
to the precedent file cabinet
the dead fish in the second draw
he called security
and the police
and he borrowed
the camera from housing
to Polaroid the decaying threat
and so for certain
he had the visual evidence
but the stench never left
and Ahern never quite caught on
that Felix regularly spat in the draw
pissed in the drawer
masturbated over the handles
of the cabinet itself
Felix beyond suspicion anyway
Ahern would never suspect
someone with a Catholic name
and about that fish?
it was a nice bass
caught in Salmon River in Dunstable
it'd been in my freezer a while though

Cornelius' gas grill

bad luck day one
who would give a guy that kind of name
and he's raising two grandchildren
because his son married inappropriately
Jezebel one two
and then this is it
he brings the propane tank
into the house for the winter
and stumbles on the cellar stair
he doesn't actually fall down the stairs
but the propane tank does
bounces down the steps
and slams onto the cement floor
the tank cracks
the propane reaches the furnace pilot light
and the house goes up
Cornelius is burnt horribly
on the arms
and this is something
two months later
the guy gets cancer of the mouth and dies
he worked til the end though
I donated four hours annual leave
toward his sick time
and I recall he said to me
or what he wrote on the routing slip
thanks a bunch
it really made me feel good
good I wasn't him

Action Johnson and the mass transit vouchers

administrator divides the alphabet by thirteen
and then designates two letter blocks
to certain half hours of his four hour workday
for those assigned to pick up vouchers
when you pick them up
he passes the time cordially
and then in passing asks
how much does it really cost you
for a bus ticket?
a prosecutorial test ha!
now sometimes
he varies things
instead of a three day period
a four day period
or he begins mid-alphabetically
and then by two letter alternate opposing pairs
goes towards the distal ends
of the alphabet
Action Johnson goes up as soon as he can
says gimme my vouchers, you silly man

she dissects

she found an owl's fur ball
under a tree in the Common
and thrilled
brought it back to the office
and you know
she said
she never threw away a book
the same with school supplies
from a marine bio course
she brought in a dissecting kit
and dissected the thing
found a rat's skull
it really grossed out Tim
at the next cube
Tim a very sensitive guy
all he could venture was
I hope you wash your hands before lunch

the wake of Moore's son

it happened the young guy fell or tripped
or dodged the wrong way
but was not pushed
off a subway platform
and swollen skull aside
the knife wound was deemed
the cause of death
the news in the office at the last minute
said you can go
but you have to sign for annual leave
so Oliver and I
are the office representatives
I have to say
we are not in the office hierarchy
and that not a single boss shows
Ollie comes over to my desk
asks to borrow my shoe polish
he says my father would be pissed
I show up at a wake needing a shoeshine
I mention at this point
you want to borrow the extra tie in my desk?
oh yeah he says
he adds my father would roll over
his casket
he knew I'm at a Roxbury wake

Lenny is out sick

he'll be out for a while
and that is all
I'm gonna say about it
it could be that
some of you know more about it
that's OK
I have no problem with that
I can say that
Len is optimistic
and that he plans
to be back but for now
all I am going to say is that
I am in contact with him
and I would tell to you
that Lenny is going to be out
for a while
thank you very much

unit chief

did I say any swear words?
this morning all I said was
did you have sex with your husband
this morning?
I don't know why
she had to get all upset
I was just making a joke
why did she have to run crying
to the ladies room?
I didn't use any bad words
or anything like that did I?
did I mention her boyfriend?

WandaMay

did anyone say I was wrong?
who said that?
that person tell me to my face
if I'm right or wrong
who want to say it?
who want tell me
to my face?
say I'm wrong
and Alvaro goes
WandaMay, Johnson said you're wrong
and Johnson is crying out loudly
IdidnotIdidnot
and Alvaro persists
he did it I heard him
why else he deny it, WandaMay?

she like silver

she like silver
and I know that wrong
and I told him
she be bad stories for him
any girl worth salt
like gold or diamonds
and she like silver
what kind of girl like silver?
someone not ever happy
not even ever content

this is it

about the new guy?
this is the thing
he misappropriates
as in you've seen
my banana label collection
stickers on bananas
I have the original collection
that exists in the office
he saw what I was doing
and he copies it
he has a collection now
and I assure you
it is not as extensive
as egregious as mine
although I am wondering how
he got so many different Ecuadors
but how can you be civil
with someone essentially a thief?
other than that he's all right

Cindi's fur coat

when no one was looking
I saw him touch a sleeve
of her coat gently
on the hanger
I don't know why he did it
I mean it wasn't mink
or anything
it looked like made
of patches
of fifty different kinds
of endangered wild rat

make a issue

I am not talking to you
but if anybody might be listening
when I working
I don't have time
look at everyone else
I just doin my own work
minding my own
you got a problem?
that your problem
thank you
maybe you talk to Queenie
you have a issue
stare at my desk
all you want
you studying at me?
talk to Queenie Beany you want
some people don't
have enough do round here
they make up a issue don't exist
thank you very much

never in a hundred years

I would never do that
I would never
ask you a question
and then
not liking your answer
go ask someone else
the very same question
albeit even though I knew
she knew the right answer
and you didn't
I would never do that
I mean I've lost
friends like that
superficial people like you

oh God, yes

she was so nice too
the kind of vegetarian
who'd use no animal products
to the extent of
plastic belts and shoes
salads were OK for her
and there's Timmy
walking by her at lunch
Timmy's saying
Mara, plants have feelings too
oh God, some day
just let me smack him
and she was so pretty
despite her being too thin
you could look at her all day
though I would try not to
sometimes I would glance at her
and then think to myself
oh God, please someday
let me buy her a sandwich

come-along

Armand in the office
the next cubical over
always bragging
about gifts from his son
a case of motor oil for Christmas
two cases of WD 40 for a birthday
and not only the quantities
but the types of gift
were unusual
a half dozen ski masks
and I was getting suspicious
with some of the presents
a locksmith tool set for Father's Day
a professional glass cutter kit
two different sizes of come-alongs
a set of wall board knives
now come-alongs are winches
used to knock down a fence
or pull down walls
or pull out windows
as one might use
to destroy a house
or break into one
the son eventually goes to jail
all kinds of burgled items
in his condo
I asked recently how's the scion doing?
post-slammer
and you know the lad is doing great
has his own business now
selling things on the internet
Armand asks me
do I need any stereo equipment?

the wall board knife

Armand's son reads
an article somewhere
unscrupulous contractors
are building houses so cheaply
with fiberboard
that any crook
can break in
not through a door or window
but just using a wall board knife
and cutting through siding
and particle board
very easily
Armand related this to me
before his son
went to the sneezer in Billerica
but I was curious
so I ask a contractor acquaintance
someone building two million dollar
condos in Concord
does he use
cheap fiberboard in construction?
right away he says no
and then he adds
not when anyone's looking

solidarity

the manager
assistant manager
admin services officer
both liaison assistants
the union president
and all three shop stewards
all now at the partnership council
quality control management seminar
on sunny Cape Cod this week
this is specifically timed
for a state convention
of commonwealth agency counterparts
a unique golf opportunity here
we are talking
let us hope
they have good weather
and that nothing real bad
happens to their balls on the Cape
rain dance begins when, Wally?

boss asks

boss asks anyone
found his balls on the Cape?
whenever the very few times
I have to make a private call
on the office phone
it seems
like this someone
is always hanging around
the one area
and that person is always listening
Kimberly called the director
wants to meet him
at the Rhino Club at seven
you come back from break
and that person is hanging around your desk
purportedly looking for a missing file
director wants somebody
get him a prune Danish
and I don't want to mention any names
but I am beginning
to leave fake messages
career enhancement notes
around for Gerard
to notice
next time he hangs
the boss wants gung ho person
to volunteer sequence check of files
from digit zero zero

the Nagant

Peter Benlian brought back
a couple of souvenirs from the war
and looking through his trunk much later
Liz thought she might try
to sell the pistol she found
she assumed it was German
it had a star on the handle
over the phone the sportsmen's club man
sounded very interested
and she arranged an appointment
she brings it in her purse
takes it out and puts it on a table
and four or five men were there
this is Russian they are saying
and they are ooing and ahhing
until Liz takes out the other souvenir
the grenade
she puts it on the table
and you never saw
people move so fast she said
they didn't touch it
they just called the bomb squad
at which time Liz
put the Nagant in her purse and left

Liz and the Chinese audience

Liz Benlian worked a second job
as an usher at various theaters
in Boston mainly the Shubert
and the Colonial
sometimes the Wilbur
so one night after the show
she's leaving
and two punks grab her purse
Liz does not let go
they knocked her down
she still does not let go
but just at that time
a Chinese Kung Fu movie
lets out its audience
mostly young Chinese men
Liz said it was really beautiful
how those nice young men moved

the people do not need modern art

for Camper Van Beethoven

how art influences people though
the statue attracts only a few tourists a day
just outside our office building
and at that time it attracts Felix
who tries to get into the photos
the background anyway
dropping his pants before the window
and processing his butt against the pane
if only a wish could break glass

the revenge of Alvaro

Alvaro returned from break
and I say to him
your wife called while you were gone
she said you don't have to call her back
because she never wants to see you again
and Alvaro goes
we even now we even

Red Line

this young man
was talking a mile a minute
and I could notice right away
that he wasn't talking to anyone
in particular
but loud so loud he was talking
to just himself he went on and on
and it was really annoying
I have to say
I finally walked up to him
and asked him what his name was
and he told me
and I forget now what it was
I used his name then and I said you
do you mind keeping quiet?
so he said OK
and he was good for five minutes
he kept quiet
but he started right up again
so I walked over again
I said you
and I used his real name
you was good for a while
try keeping quiet again
and sure enough he was good
the rest of the trip
isn't that something though?
I can't seem to recall his name now
and if I see him again
I'll have to start all over

last meeting with Robin

she goes
when you asked three times asked
for the tally sheets you didn't say it nicely
you didn't like ask us
you were too forceful
you were accusing us
all of us
why don't you just talk privately
to the person
who didn't turn in
the tally sheets the last three times?
he goes
because that person was you, Robin
she goes
oh that's funny
that's very funny hahaha
but that's not true
and she leaves
giving him a mean look
and then winking at me
when she leaves
and he says to me then
privately
I had my way
they wouldn't hire
any women here
at all never
adding very forcefully
never ever

assurance for building workers

there have been several inquiries
about the safety
of the building elevators
since last week
when a blind man
fell in the shaft
of elevator two in the high rise
his dog would not go into the shaft
and stayed outside
and the blind man
pulled so hard
in his fall
the harness broke
the contractor was called
and has inspected the system
and found nothing
is wrong with the system
we thank everyone for her concern
and appreciate all questions made
and want all building employees
to know
that the dog was not harmed

6

funeral coffee tea

my stepmother called
regarding arrangements
for my dad's funeral
she is actually my second stepmother
and she wanted to do things informally
in a manner that my dad would have liked
you should understand
that this stepmother
is two years
younger than I am
and that she is very cute
well this was it
the funeral banquet
will be in the church hall
but it won't just be
coffee tea and cookies
it would be coffee tea and
my dad's favorite sandwich
peanut butter and bananas
what could I say
it's true I said
that that was his favorite sandwich
but
his favorite meal was steak and lobster
and it was a dead silence
the other end of the phone

my current building site

understand this is not an old building
being refurbished
this is a new structure
an actual complex of several buildings
for tall condos
the largest of which eight stories
assisted living for the elderly
and if something went wrong
nobody could ever get grandma
out of the top floors
and before we are done
the homeless are moving in
now you guess what reason
look up the word cheap
the bosses aren't hiring security
to keep them away
and I know they are there
but I am not searching every room
every floor to find them out
how I know they exist?
from the spots on the parking lot
designated residential parking whereat
the homeless leave their grocery carts
they're over there
it's pretty neatly done

electric eyes

usually a building site
has a night time security
a retired cop or someone
with a German shepherd
but not this place
my first thought the builders too cheap
and too foolish
but get this there's a bank next door
that has security up the alley
five electric eyes at each corner
plus ones on the sides of the bank
yeah lots of electric eyes
why so many views at the corners?
there's left right
up down
in out
well six actually
my site's contractors
feel our place covered
the homeless don't think so
nor does my brother Jimmy

girl the next house over

I liked her my neighbor
and she liked me at one time
but I was at a movie
with someone else
and saw my neighbor
and did not say hello
later on a neighborhood walk
I saw her and apologized
I said I have no social poise
or rather have that of a field mouse
and I should have
introduced you to my date
but I confessed
I was a nervous wreck
then because I was expecting
to see my date's husband any minute
and the girl next door
never spoke to me again
whatsoever her reasons

me rough me tough

Veterans' Day
Eddie asks me
where was it you got hit?
I tell him frankly I wasn't hit
I say to him
I was rear echelon
I gave out speeding tickets
on Highway One
I say the worst thing
it wasn't
for me there
was the heat
Eddie nods and says
those islands are all alike

"Day to Day"

neighbors three streets over
were talking saying
it was a great neighborhood
until people from Lowell moved in
I am from Lowell
and my hair lifted
and then they say
it's the Burgess family
and I understood
the Bourgeois family
well known in Lowell
you shake hands with one
you count your fingers after
the *Lowell Sun*'s
police log "Day to Day"
had the family as regulars
and soon enough
a scion of the Bourgeois family
is in the town soccer league
with my son
and it is Jesse James Bourgeois
on the other side
making a penalty kick
my son is goalie
Jesse kicks a bullet
straight to Sean
who catches it easily
and in a display
of sportsmanship yells HAH
Jesse yells back you're dead, Sean
and Sean yells back
I'm scared, Jesse, I'm scared

North Main Street

for Douglas Dunn

he is walking back and forth
in front of the old town hall
his placard is cardboard
maybe three by four feet
colored red electric blue and yellow
the colors of the local pizza place
and he's holding it
so it hides his face
he is wearing a hat of sorts
with an umbrella top
of the same colors
same same his shirt
I walk by and he is on a cell phone
and from behind the placard
and from under the hat
I hear him
yeah yeah I am working downtown now
his placard reads
for a very short time
only
a very large pizza
four toppings
just four ninety-nine
phone in your order now
he says
yeah yeah I am in promotions now
I stop quickly
write down the phone number

drivers ed

it was my mother's fault
she messed up the application thing
and so I had to take
the classroom drivers ed sessions twice
and it was unbelievably boring
the first time around
but the second session
had the cheerleaders in it
junior varsity
and they'd show up from practice
in uniform including get this
the girl with the broken leg in a cast
out of solidarity I guess
actually she was the one
who liked strawberry spritzers
she was all right really
and her car always smelled good

CHEERS

a girl in my driver's ed class
a cheerleader how do I know?
she would wear her cheerleader outfit
to class JV sometimes with sweats
you know how some of the girls
have the word CHEER
across their butt
this particular girl
had CHEER CHEER
a cheer for each side
my honest opinion
she was very nice
I have to say it
she had one brown eye
and one blue eye
and she looked really good
like a mis-minted coin golden

pumpkin family

family nearby
before every Thanksgiving
would have a like family
of pumpkins
all smiles
together on the front step
mother father daughter son
and this was every year
until the kids
were both through college
and the father was
through with the family
through with the wife anyway
so the next year's Halloween
there's only two pumpkins
on the front step
not together anymore
they're on each corner of the top step
and one of the pumpkins
is visibly damaged
not like it was dropped
but more like
its face was kicked in
you could not even see his smile

diction a detriment to the working class

she used to be our neighbor
but they moved away to a bigger house
and I babysat when she was nearby
one child then
and I babysat when she moved
two children later
to a monster house
three car garage
into none of which
would the Hummer fit
she knew the going rate
one dollar per hour per child
she always rounded down
one hour fifteen minutes
would be paid as one hour
it grated though
but jobs are jobs
so I get the call one day
they drove me there and back
and while there
her aunt shows
with her four children
I am there
for three hours twenty minutes
and she gave me three big ones
next time she called
I declined and she was really mad
I mean I was the one cheated
you know that right?
however in retrospect
I should not have said
fuck you and your auntie too
well I guess

once employed

I thought I'd improve
our living standard
send the wife out get a job
she's getting up in age
into the indefinable fifties
and she calls it lower mid
and she and I
are thinking retirement
as in she needs
social security quarters
so she starts working
this very summer
part time
and it is witching and moaning
all the while
all summer long
and finally
around September twenty-first
she has earnings worth one quarter
such that her total quarters
not just for the summer
but for her entire lifetime
employment history
is one quarter
once one gets into
the indefinable fifties
mid fifties
it's time you know

Halloween tennis

I am trick or treating
with the neighborhood
children and dads
at one house
a mom appears at the door
in a tennis outfit
ordered from
fertility goddess dot com
think Adriana La Cerva
from *The Sopranos*
and the dad I am with
dashes up the stairs to chat
on the way to the next house
he asks
do you know who she is?
I say Courtney's mom now divorced
no he says that's half
forty million

Thanksgiving

at the mother-in-law's
this a month after her husband's death
she is still ripping
that my son did not go to the wake
it was our call after all
the kid is only seven
but it bothers the mother-in-law
Thanksgiving
seven times she mentioned it to my hearing
how she was surprised
that the kid was not there
she ignores the fact that the boy
the next day
at the funeral at the cemetery
where everyone froze his ass
I mean this was seven times
within my ears' hearing
she obsesses over this
and I was out of the room somewhiles
during which she must have complained
I was good all the time
I didn't say a word
but at the end of the visit
at the door saying goodbye
she again states I cannot get over
my dismay that his own grandson
was not at his grandfather's wake
you know what I says
he won't be at yours either

Thanksgiving 2

my friend Phil looks around the table
and says to everyone
while looking at me
don't you think it's funny
that none of your kids
came home Thanksgiving
I could not think of anything to say
but later on commented
that I was glad
the nursing home
allowed hospice to care
for Phil's mom in the nursing home
and it was too bad
Phil couldn't visit his mom
on Thanksgiving
I did acknowledge out loud
that the nursing home was far away
up in New Hampshire
over the line and would a been
at least a twenty minute ride
twenty minutes
altogether to and fro
point A to point B
like the door opens see

the distance to one's wit's end

she exaggerates
and she's an actress
and also she's loud
Fourth of July
my stepmother calls
this my second stepmother
very like a Kewpie doll
she is frantic
she's hysterical
my father fainted and he won't
go to the doctor or the hospital
or anything
OK I says I'll talk to him
oh that is great that'll really help
put him on the phone
no she can't do that
why? because he went to the liquor store
well when did he faint?
Memorial Day she says
she's at her wit's end
that's a short journey I says
the liquor store is not far
just make sure
you have orange juice in the house
for when he gets dizzy
I'll call back in a couple months
you know he actually left my mother
for such an earlier beaut

Bibliography

BOOKS

Obscenities
Yale University Press, 1972; Warner Paperback Library, 1972;
Ashod Press, 1990; Carnegie Melon University Press, 2002

Millrat
Adastra Press, 1999

The Million Dollar Hole
Orchises Press, 2001

Check Points
Adastra Press, 2011

CHAPBOOKS

Millrat
Adastra Press, 1996

Untitled accordion booklet
Longhouse, 2001

Raiding a Whorehouse
Adastra Press, 2004

Permanent Party
March Street Press, 2005

Cindi's Fur Coat
The Chuckwagon, 2006

The Bopper
Kendra Steiner Editions, 2007

The Wall Board Knife
Kendra Steiner Editions, 2011

Notes

Names, terms, and abbreviations are defined on their first appearance in the text.

1

THE LAST YANKEE: Uncollected. Line 1, Centralville: a neighborhood in Lowell, Massachusetts.

GRANDFATHER'S PHOTOGRAPH: Uncollected.

THE MARLBOROUGH: Uncollected.

SOLID STATE PHYSICS: Uncollected.

RELATIVITY: Uncollected.

MY LANDLADY'S DAUGHTER: Uncollected.

RUM DRUNK: Uncollected.

EARLY MORNING BEFORE THE OPTICS FINAL: Uncollected.

GETTING SO: from *Millrat*.

MY BROTHER THE HELPER: Uncollected.

LOWELL POEM: Uncollected.

MARYANN: Uncollected.

GLAZED: Uncollected.

GOLF OUTING: Uncollected.

SEVERED HEAD: Uncollected.

BEAUTIFUL DAY: Uncollected.

BLUE DOT SIGN: Uncollected.

LOWELL SUN "DAY TO DAY": Uncollected. Title, lines 6, 19, 30, *Lowell Sun*: daily newspaper of Lowell, Massachusetts; line 3, Portygee: Portuguese; line 12, Khmer: Cambodian.

TAYLOR'S PINK CATAWBA: Uncollected.

MY ELECTRONICS COMPANY: Uncollected.

2

DRIVING WHILE UNDER THE INFLUENCE: from *Millrat*. Line 3, Drum Hill: location in Chelmsford, Massachusetts.

THE COMPANY POOL: from *Millrat*. Line 12, *The Record*: Boston newspaper which evolved into *Boston Herald*.

FOREMAN: from *Millrat*.
DYE HOUSE: from *Millrat*.

SAME GUY AGAIN: from *Millrat*.

WALTER'S SORE FEET: from *Millrat*.

COFFEE TRUCK: from *Millrat*.

THE NIGHT THE FIGHT WITH BILL HAPPENED: from *Millrat*.

BREAK ROOM: from *Millrat*.

JUST ONE B & E: from *Millrat*. Title & line 4, B & E: criminal offense of breaking and entering.

MAINTENANCE: from *Millrat*.

FORKLIFT DRIVER: from *Millrat*. Line 17, napping: textile mill treatment to raise the surface of cloth.

DESERT BOOTS: from *Millrat*.

MY YOUNGEST THAT TALL: from *Millrat*.

MILL NEWS: from *Millrat*.

3

THE COMPANY PHYSICAL COMBAT PROFICIENCY TEST AVERAGE: from *Obscenities*.

TO SERGEANT ROCK: from *Obscenities*.

MAIN GATE: from *The Million Dollar Hole*.

RIOT CONTROL SCHOOL: from *Obscenities*. Line 5, Walter Mitty: fictional character in James Thurber's short story, "The Secret Life of Walter Mitty," who envisions himself in various adventures.

OUTPATIENT CLINIC, GENERAL WOOD HOSPITAL: from *The Million Dollar Hole*. Line 1, provost marshal: military police chief of an army base or unit; line 2, OPC: outpatient clinic.

MASTRANTONIO AND THE RHINOCEROS BEETLE: from *The Million Dollar Hole.*

PACO: from *Obscenities.* Line 8, ten-twenty: radio code for "disregard"; line 8, ten-twenty-four: radio code for "assignment"; line 11, dust: money.

MANWARRING'S DEFENESTRATION: from *The Million Dollar Hole.* Line 6, turnkey: prison guard in charge of door or gate; line 7, sally port: entrance and exit gate of an army stockade (prison).

SERIOUS INCIDENT REPORT: MALTREATMENT OF TRAINEE: from *Obscenities.* Title, Serious Incident Report: police report, such as "Theft of a Weapon," sent to Pentagon; line 4, willies: trainees.

SIERRA TANGO: from *Obscenities.* Title, sierra tango: words in the phonetic radio alphabet representing letters S and T, creating an acronym for "stick time," a euphemism for clubbing; line 7, Mike Papa: words in the phonetic radio alphabet representing letters M and P, creating an acronym for "military police."

GUARDMOUNT SPEECH: from *Obscenities.* Title, guardmount: inspection and briefing of stockade guards at the beginning of a shift; lines 18 & 22, duty officer: officer in charge of shift.

ONE LIFEGUARD, RESCUED: from *The Million Dollar Hole.* Line 4, WAC: Women's Army Corps.

GIFT RABBIT: from *Permanent Party.* Line 1, white hat: military police; line 1, Fort Wood: Fort Leonard Wood, Missouri; line 3, NCO: non-commissioned officer.

CHURCH KEY: from *The Million Dollar Hole.*

TEN-TEN THE AREA: from *The Million Dollar Hole.* Title, ten-ten: radio code for "patrol."

MY BROTHER-IN-LAW AND ME: from *The Million Dollar Hole.*

DAVIS AND THE LION: from *The Million Dollar Hole.*

THE BEAR: from *The Million Dollar Hole.*

CRASH SHATTER: from *The Million Dollar Hole.* Line 12, MP: military police; line 17, pees: military police.

THE HOGTIEING OF MONTGOMERY: from *The Million Dollar Hole.* Title, hogtieing: immobilizing rope restraint; line 1, Villa: Pancho

Villa, Mexican general; line 12, white hats: military policemen.

WARREN IN THE RYE: from *Permanent Party*.

FRISK: from *Permanent Party*.

463RD MILITARY POLICE COMPANY, ESCORT GUARD: from *Permanent Party*. Line 1, mess steward: sergeant in charge of the mess (dining facility); line 9, permanent party: regularly stationed cadre at an army fort; line 13, Duster: Dodge car model.

COOKIES OUT OF HUMOR: from *Permanent Party*.

WHICHWAYDIDHEGO WHICHWAYDIDHEGO: from *Permanent Party*. Line 2, OJT: on-the-job training.

LAST PATROL: from *Permanent Party*. Line 8, adjutant general: legal officer of army unit, & levy section: adjutant general department in charge of troop assignments; line 26, white hats: hats worn by military police on duty.

4

LEARNING: from *Obscenities*.

WELCOME: from *Obscenities*.

A BUMMER: from *Obscenities*. Line 4, track: vehicle with tracks, not wheels—in this case an armored personnel carrier; line 7, TC: track commander.

MESSAGE IN THE PUBLIC INTEREST: from *Obscenities*. Line 25, Monkey Mountain: Son Tra Mountain, Central Vietnam.

SEVEN LETTERS FOR HARMON: from *Check Points*.

DOG CEMETERY: from *Check Points*.

SHOTGUN RIDE: from *Check Points*. Line 2, steel pot: helmet; line 3, bandolier: cloth belt worn over shoulder and across chest, with pockets for bullet magazines; line 4, brassard: armband; line 5, flak jacket: armored vest.

THE DEATH TRUCK: from *Obscenities*.

SHOTGUN RIDER TWO: from *Check Points*. Line 22, *khong the duoc*: "cannot do," Vietnamese.

JOHN ON JEEP HOOD: from *Check Points*.

JOHN AND THE KALASHNIKOV: Uncollected. Title, Kalashnikov: Russian weapon designer, synonymous with the AK-47; line 2, hooch: barracks; line 5, AK-47: Soviet Russian-designed automatic assault rifle.

SNIPER: from *Check Points*. Line 2, Ruger: firearm manufacturer, here referring to a rifle; lines 26 & 31, *im*: "quiet," Vietnamese.

RAIDING A WHOREHOUSE: from *Check Points*. *sin thay xe jip*: "please watch the jeep," Vietnamese; ruffpuffs: South Vietnamese regional popular force militiamen; *gai diem*: "prostitute," Vietnamese; ETS: end tour of service; John P. Fogarty: reference to John C. Fogarty—singer, guitarist, and songwriter for rock and roll group Creedence Clearwater Revival.

DEPLOY DEPLOY: Uncollected. Line 1, LZ: landing zone, army base with a helicopter landing zone; line 2, BTOC: brigade tactical operation center.

THE LZ GATOR BODY COLLECTOR: from *Obscenities*.

ON DEATH: from *Obscenities*.

OFFICERS CLUB: from *Check Points*. Line 3, Stanley: provost marshal's security matron, nicknamed after comic actor Stanley Laurel.

POEM FOR MARY TYLER MOORE: from *Check Points*.

VICTOR: from *Check Points*. Line 1, Victor November: words in the phonetic radio alphabet representing letters V and N, signifying "Vietnamese."

DOWNTOWN RESIDENTIAL AN TAN: from *Check Points*. Lines 3 & 5, *may gio ruoui*: "what time is it?," Vietnamese.

SERGEANT LE'S WATCH: from *Check Points*.

CENERIZIO'S SERVICE: from *Check Points*. Line 5, cage: prisoner of war camp; line 8, ARVN: acronym for Army of the Republic of South Vietnam, & QC: Vietnamese acronym for *quan canh*, "military police"; line 12, Chu Lai: seaport, home to a large American military base; line 17, monkey house: prisoner of war camp.

PERSONAL EFFECTS: from *Check Points*. Line 3, orange malaria pills: large malaria pill with a disagreeable side effect; line 4, white malaria pills: small malaria pill for daily use; line 5, Americal Division: large army division, troops from which committed the My Lai massacre.

BAGLEY REMOVES A THOUGHT: from *Check Points*.

PENTAGON: from *Check Points*. Line 1, My Lai tragedy: March 1968 killing of hundreds of unarmed civilians in the hamlet of My Lai; line 3, Seymour Hersh: acclaimed American journalist who exposed the My Lai massacre; lines 3-4, Seymour Hersh story / on Ky Chanh: Hersh wrote on the July 1969 killing of ten civilians in the village of Ky Chanh, by Americal Division helicopter pilots, for *The New Yorker* in October 1971; line 7, Highway One: highway that runs the length of Vietnam.

CAP SAINT-JACQUES: from *Check Points*. Title, Cap Saint-Jacques: cape in southern Vietnam.

5

SHE: from *The Bopper*.

YOU STINK AS A BOSS: from *The Bopper*.

SUMMER SIZZLER OUTFIT: Uncollected.

MISTER AHERN: from *The Bopper*. Line 26, Dunstable: rural town in northeastern Massachusetts.

CORNELIUS' GAS GRILL: Uncollected.

ACTION JOHNSON AND THE MASS TRANSIT VOUCHERS: from *Cindi's Fur Coat*.

SHE DISSECTS: from *The Bopper*. Line 2, the Common: Boston Common, central park of Boston, Massachusetts.

THE WAKE OF MOORE'S SON: Uncollected. Line 25, Roxbury: predominantly Black neighborhood of Boston.

LENNY IS OUT SICK: from *The Bopper*.

UNIT CHIEF: from *Cindi's Fur Coat*.

WANDAMAY: from *Cindi's Fur Coat*.

SHE LIKE SILVER: Uncollected.

THIS IS IT: Uncollected.

CINDI'S FUR COAT: from *Cindi's Fur Coat*.

MAKE A ISSUE: from *Cindi's Fur Coat*.

NEVER IN A HUNDRED YEARS: from *Cindi's Fur Coat*.

OH GOD, YES: from *Cindi's Fur Coat*.

COME-ALONG: from *The Wall Board Knife*.

THE WALL BOARD KNIFE: from *The Wall Board Knife*. Line 15, sneezer in Billerica: Middlesex Jail and House of Correction in Billerica, Massachusetts; line 19, Concord: wealthy town in eastern Massachusetts.

SOLIDARITY: from *Cindi's Fur Coat*. Line 9, Cape Cod: ocean resort area of Massachusetts.

BOSS ASKS: Uncollected.

THE NAGANT: Uncollected. Title & last line, Nagant: French-designed, Russian-manufactured firearm.

LIZ AND THE CHINESE AUDIENCE: Uncollected.

THE PEOPLE DO NOT NEED MODERN ART: from *Cindi's Fur Coat*. Line 2, the statue: Dimitri Hadzi's *Thermopylae*, a sculpture near the John F. Kennedy Federal Building in Boston's Government Center.

THE REVENGE OF ALVARO: Uncollected.

RED LINE: Uncollected. Title, Red Line: Boston subway line.

LAST MEETING WITH ROBIN: Uncollected.

ASSURANCE FOR BUILDING WORKERS: Uncollected.

6
FUNERAL COFFEE TEA: Uncollected.

MY CURRENT BUILDING SITE: Uncollected.

ELECTRIC EYES: Uncollected.

GIRL THE NEXT HOUSE OVER: Uncollected.

ME ROUGH ME TOUGH: Uncollected.

"DAY TO DAY": Uncollected.

NORTH MAIN STREET: Uncollected.

DRIVERS ED: Uncollected.

CHEERS: Uncollected.

PUMPKIN FAMILY: Uncollected.

DICTION A DETRIMENT TO THE WORKING CLASS: Uncollected. Line 10, Hummer: brand of truck.

ONCE EMPLOYED: Uncollected.

HALLOWEEN TENNIS: Uncollected. Lines 9-10, Adriana La Cerva / from *The Sopranos*: Adriana La Cerva is a fictional character in the HBO television show *The Sopranos*.

THANKSGIVING: Uncollected.

THANKSGIVING 2: Uncollected.

THE DISTANCE TO ONE'S WIT'S END: Uncollected. Line 7, Kewpie doll: small doll given out at carnivals and circuses.

About the Author

Michael Casey is from Lowell, Massachusetts, and attended the public schools in that city. He received a B.S. degree in physics in 1968 from University of Massachusetts-Lowell, where poet William Aiken taught the modern poetry course. Drafted that year, Casey became a military policeman in Fort Leonard Wood, Missouri, and later in Landing Zone Bayonet, Quang Ngai Province, Vietnam, with the Americal Division. The journal of his military experience became the book *Obscenities*, published in 1972 by Yale University Press. His book *Millrat*, on blue collar work in a textile mill dye house, has been published by Adastra Press. Casey taught for many years at Northern Essex Community College in Haverhill, Massachusetts.